Prepper's Pantry

The Survival Guide to Emergency Water & Food Storage

By Ron Johnson

Disclaimer

This book is intended to be a general guide, to raise awareness, and to help people make informed decisions in the context of their own personal circumstance.

The author accepts no responsibility for any loss or injury be it personal or financial, as a result for the use or misuse of the information in this book. If you have any doubts or concerns after reading this book, please speak to a qualified person before taking any actions.

Contents

Introduction

Chapter 1
How to Plan For the Short, Medium & Long Term

Chapter 2
How to Safely and Efficiently Store Water

Chapter 3
How to Safely and Efficiently Store Food

Chapter 4
How to Can Your Fresh Food and Other Ways of Preserving Your Fresh Food

Chapter 5
Strategies to Help You Properly Manage Your Food and Water In The Event Of an Emergency

Chapter 6
How to Effectively Scavenge and Restock Your Supplies

Conclusion

Introduction

Oxygen, Shelter, Sleep, Food and Water are the basic needs of all humans to survive. Have you been in a situation that one of these is not accessible? How does it feel? For instance, have you tried holding your breath for a minute or so? It feels like dying, right? How about, not drinking water for a day or two? You probably feel like you are going to thirst to death. Just try to imagine not having shelter during the rainy season, or winter. Do you think you will pull through it? Probably not. Planning and preparing are vital, so reading this book is your guide to survival.

Types of Emergencies

Natural calamities like earthquakes, volcanic eruptions, landslides, flash floods, severe storms, hurricanes and power shortages are only some of the possible emergencies we may encounter any day of the year. Imagine that the authorities will tell you to evacuate in ten minutes. The stores are all closed because of the severe situation in your community, and there are no means for you to buy food, or water for your family. What will you do now? Will you be able to gather enough resources to help you and your entire family during these emergencies? If you answer yes, then how sure are you that it would be enough.

Hurricane Katrina is a good example of a major catastrophic event which can have a massive impact and can occur with little warning

Be Prepared for an Emergency

Most of us seem to prepare for emergencies only when it is time to face one. We never recognize the importance of being prepared at all times. Being prepared takes us to different stages of knowing when to act and  how to act appropriately in the case of emergencies.

This book will provide essential tips on how to properly plan, organize and prepare for future emergencies. Read, learn and get all the tips you need to survive!!!

Chapter 1

How Plan For the Short, Medium & Long Term

Planning for Emergencies

Sometimes, it goes without saying "Prevention is better than cure." It is indeed, true. When you have planned what to do, it makes things easier for you to organize your resources. Please bear in mind that it's always better to have it, even if you don't need it, than to need it, but you totally don't have it. Emergencies always happen every time we don't expect them.

There are things that we need to consider in starting our emergency food pantry. Consider the shelf life of the food; you don't want to end up eating a rotten or spoiled food in order to survive right? You also need consider that the stored food you have is enough to sustain your entire family; you don't want to see their hungry faces during these situations, do you? On top of that, it is a must to consider what to store, how to store it, and how much you do need to store.

Short Term Emergencies

Short term emergencies are those emergencies that last at least a day up to a couple of weeks. Planning for such emergencies is not as meticulous as planning for long term ones.

Water and food storage during this type of emergencies should be quickly accessed. Find food and water that can supply you and your family with enough energy for several days. Bear in mind that a person needs a gallon of drinking water each and every day. Water should never be compromised at any times. A certain individual can last a maximum of ten days without drinking water, starting at 26° Celsius; your life span decreases a day every time the temperature increases by 5 degrees. You don't want to see your family slowly dying just because of thirst or dehydration.

Chosen foods should be those that are ready–to–eat without the need of cooking, re-heating or refrigeration, because the electricity might be shut off. You don't want to end up eating raw foods. Commercially, canned foods are the best choices, since they do not require cooking or refrigeration.

During short-term emergencies, you should look for calories and comfort foods. Are you aware of what comfort foods are? Comfort foods are high in carbohydrates, and it is exactly what your body will need. While dealing with an emergency situation, do not worry about vitamins or nutrients you will not receive for a short period. If any family members have any health issues, make sure you don't forget any medicines or special foods they may need during an emergency. Don't forget, if you have a baby, then please make sure you have an elaborate plan to keep the milk from spoiling. You never want to see your baby crying due to an empty stomach, right?

Medium Term Emergencies

Medium term emergencies are those, which can last from three weeks to three months. These type of emergencies where food and water supply can be interrupted for various reasons. Hurricane Katrina is one perfect example of emergency where roads are inaccessible, thus making it hard for relief goods to enter the community.

When you are preparing for emergency situations, try to gather foods that are part of your daily diet. These should not be all canned goods. You can purchase cases of water, grains, cereals, beans and powdered milk. You may start buying some of these items weekly until you finally reach your goal. You can also try to do homemade preservation of foods like drying of fish and fruits, etc. for medium emergencies. You should look for calorie-rich foods and at least find time to sustain the daily nutrients your body needs. We will discuss the homemade preservation later in the book.

Long Term Emergencies

Long term emergencies are those types of emergencies that could last from few months to a year. These types of emergencies may happen less often, but it is still better to be prepared just in case it might occur.

Long term food supplies can be a mixture of canned goods and low moisture foods that can last for several of months or years. Be sure though, that you get all the nutrients you need during the whole duration of the emergency.

That next thing that you need to consider is the amount that you need to secure for your entire family; we will be doing some math here. It is just a suggested amount per person per year.

For Family Members AGES 0-6

Grains	Legumes	Sugars	Fats and Oils	Cooking Essentials	Milk
12 Lbs. Of Pasta	1 Lbs. Of Split Peas	1 Lbs. Of Brown Sugar	2 Lbs. Of Peanut Butter	1 Lbs. Baking Soda	6 Cans Of Evaporated Milk
12 Lbs. Of Oats	1 Lbs. Of Lentils	1 Lbs. Of Honey	2 Lbs. Of Shortening	0.5 Lbs. Yeast	30 Lbs. Of Dry Milk
12 Lbs. Of Corn Meal	1 Lbs. Of Lima Beans	1 Lbs. Of Corn Syrup	1 Qt. Of Salad Dressing	3 Lbs. Salt	6 Lbs. Of Other Milk Desired
12 Lbs. Of Flour	1 Lbs. Of Dry Soup Mix	1 Lbs. Jam	1 Gal. Of Vegetable Oil	0.5 Lbs. Vinegar	
25 Lbs. Of Rice	5 Lbs. Of Soy Beans	1 Lbs. Molasses	1 Qt. Of Mayonnaise	1 Lbs. Baking Powder	
75 Lbs. Of Wheat	15 Lbs. Of Dried Beans	1 Lbs. Flavored Gelatin			
		3 Lbs. Powdered Fruit Drink			
		20 Lbs. Of Sugar			
TOTAL GRAINS: 148 Lbs.	TOTAL LEGUMES: 24 Lbs.	TOTAL SUGAR: 29 Lbs.	TOTAL FATS AND OIL: 7 Lbs.	TOTAL CE: 6 Lbs.	TOTAL DAIRY: 37 Lbs.

For Family Ages 7+

Grains	Legumes	Sugars	Fats and Oils	Cooking Essentials	Milk
25 Lbs. Of Pasta	5 Lbs. Of Split Peas	3 Lbs. Of Brown Sugar	4 Lbs. Of Peanut Butter	1 Lbs. Baking Soda	12 Cans Of Evaporated Milk
25 Lbs. Of Oats	5 Lbs. Of Lentils	3 Lbs. Of Honey	4 Lbs. Of Shortening	0.5 Lbs. Yeast	60 Lbs. Of Dry Milk
25 Lbs. Of Corn Meal	5 Lbs. Of Lima Beans	3 Lbs. Of Corn Syrup	1 Qt. Of Salad Dressing	5 Lbs. Salt	13 Lbs. Of Other Milk Desired
25 Lbs. Of Flour	5 Lbs. Of Dry Soup Mix	3 Lbs. Jam	2 Gals. Of Vegetable Oil	0.5 Gal. Vinegar	
50 Lbs. Of Rice	10 Lbs. Of Soy Beans	1 Lbs. Molasses	2 Qtrs. Of Mayonnaise	1 Lbs. Baking Powder	
150 Lbs. Of Wheat	30 Lbs. Of Dried Beans	1 Lbs. Flavored Gelatin			
		6 Lbs. Powdered Fruit Drink			
		40 Lbs. Of Sugar			
TOTAL GRAINS: 300 Lbs.	TOTAL LEGUMES: 60 Lbs.	TOTAL SUGAR: 60 Lbs.	TOTAL FATS AND OIL: 13 Lbs.	TOTAL CE: 0.5 Lbs.	TOTAL DAIRY: 75 Lbs.

Note: 1 Gal. of water per person a day. Excluding any other activities that need water like cooking, etc.

Other Tips of Planning for Emergencies

Buy foods that you enjoy – you don't want eating foods that you really don't like, because you might end up not eating at all.

Slowly buy your food supply each week until you reach your goal. It is better to buy extra foods every single time you go for groceries, so it is no point for you to spend big amount of money all at one time.

Plan meals – it's better to plan your preferred meals during emergencies, in that way you'll know what you'll be needing in terms of ingredients and as well as the utensils. Also make a list of meals that you will serve and labelled Day 1, Day 2 up to Day 14. And if the foods are not in one location, might as well indicate where the food is.

Stock foods are high in calories and nutrients, unlike junk foods. Have on hand cooking utensils, plates, spoons and forks, etc. – it's pretty obvious, you don't want to end up eating with your bare hands, do you?

Avoid high protein, fatty and salty foods if your water supply is low. – These foods will give you a feeling of wanting more water, well that's totally fine, but in some situations like this, you have to be a little thrifty with your stored water.

Stock water in huge containers, each person should have one gallon per day.

Write down your family members names, including your pets and indicate any special needs (allergies, diabetes etc.).

List down all the consumable foods in your shelves now - you should indicate the amount available; date purchased, date opened and who used it. Post this list near storage closets or cabinets and always update when changes occur.

List all staple foods in your freezer now - you should indicate the amount available; date purchased, date opened and who used it. Post this list near storage closets or cabinets and always update when changes occur.

Make a note to each day's list that will indicate the equipment, utensils and the amount of water for the preparation. – In this manner you will be able to know what else you need to buy.

Always make sure that the food purchased is not yet expired or will not expire within the next few years – you don't want to end up eating expired foods or eating nothing at all.

Have hand sanitizer – this will keep your hands clean, and it will also help prevent you from sickness.

Have pets? – make sure you also have an allocated food for them for the entire emergency period

Chapter 2

How to Safely and Efficiently Store Water

Conserving Your Water Supply

After an emergency, water supply may not be as available as it used to be during regular days. Water sources may also be affected and are not advisable to for consumption. These tips below will teach you how to conserve properly and store your water supply in preparation for emergencies.

Prepare an Emergency Water Supply

You also need to consider how to prepare your emergency water supply. Stock up at least a gallon of drinking water for each person per day and also don't forget the water for your pets in the family. Consider storing more amount of water for hot climates, pregnant women and sick members of the family.

Rotate your drinking water supplies every 6-12 months. Observe the expiration of store-bought water to make sure it is safe to consume. If possible, replace them every six months. Unopened commercially bought water is still the safest and most dependable source of water supply. You can buy containers in surplus stores and store the water yourself. Be sure to find containers that can be shut tightly, not allowing anything to go into the stored water. Avoid containers that can break such as glass bottles. Label the containers. Label drinking water containers with "Drinking Water" and other containers can be labelled "For Other Water Purposes". Keep the water stored in cool, dry place. Do not store containers that face direct sunlight. Do not store containers near toxic liquids such as gasoline, etc. you don't want wasting water during this period, so might as well be precautions in storing your water. Water is life.

Plan water supplies for instant oatmeal, instant pudding, dried soups, dry milk, powdered drink mixes, bouillon cubes or powder, instant rice and instant potatoes.

Remember to keep a bottle of unscented household chlorine bleach that will be the disinfecting agent for your water as well as for cleaning and sanitizing another stuff.

Keeping Your Water Safe

How can you make sure that the water you've stored is safe for human consumption? What you are aiming for during emergency situation is your survival, and you don't want your survival rate to decrease just because of your intake of unsafe or contaminated water. In this section, we will teach you on how to keep your water safe from any contaminants.

Boiling water is a popular and effective way to kill bacteria BUT this not always viable where gas or electricity is not available and can really deplete your emergency wood, kerosene or propane supplies

First, you can boil water to make it safe. Boiling kills disease-causing organisms such as viruses and bacteria. You can also purify your water using unscented chlorine bleach or iodine. You can purify water by filtering it through a clean cloth, a coffee filter or paper towel then allow it to settle. Then, draw off the clear water. To use bleach add eight drops of the unscented liquid household chlorine (5-6%) bleach per gallon of clear water (or for every quart of water you can add two drops of bleach). Stir the mixture well.

Leave it around 30 to 40 minutes or longer before consumption. Store all your disinfected water in a clean and sanitized container with a tight cover.

To use iodine, follow the manufacturer's instructions. Commercial bottled water which are unopened is the safest and the most reliable emergency water supply.

The following are steps on how you can clean and sanitize your water containers before filling them up.

→ Using a dishwashing soap and water, wash the water storage container, and make sure you rinse it completely with clean water. There is no sense of washing the water bottle if after all you'll just be rinsing it with dirty or contaminated water.

→ Make a solution by simply mixing a teaspoon of the unscented liquid household chlorine bleach in a quart of water; use it to sanitize the container.

→ Cover the container and shake it well and make sure that the solution touches all the inside surfaces of the container.

→ After 30 seconds, pour the sanitizing solution out of the container.

→ Air dry the empty sanitized container before use, or you can also rinse your empty water containers with clean and safe water which is already available.

If there are safe water bottles, there are also containers that you need to avoid.

→ You have to avoid containers that can break such as glass bottles. Storing water in glass containers is not a smart idea.

→ You have to refrain from using containers that can't be tightly sealed. There is no sense of cleaning and sanitizing your water bottles if you will just be using containers that cannot be tightly sealed. It's like giving an easy access for the contaminants to contaminate your water.

→ Never use a container used for any liquid or solid chemicals (this include bleach containers).

→ Cardboard or plastic bottles, jugs and containers used for fruit juices or milk are not advisable.

Choosing the right container and preparing it in a proper way is the key to a safe emergency water supply.

Chapter 3

How to Safely and Efficiently Store Food

Safeguarding Your Food Supply

As you consider what foods to store, you also need to find a place perfect to store your foods, especially stock food, which is a part of your everyday routine and diet.

Make a list of all the foodstuffs, foods for your pet, supplies for your pet, medical needs and nutritional items. In short, prepare everything that you think you will need when forced to stay at home for several weeks or months. Decide how you'll store food, whether by kind or period. Rotating your stock is a crucial aspect of the plan, your storage areas will help you to find the best way to organize your goods.

How to choose the right container for storing your emergency foods?

Sometimes, choosing the right type and size of containers for your emergency foods, can be a little sometimes confusing. On this portion, we will help you with some beneficial information that you need to know when storing your emergency foods.

→ Always make sure to use a food grade container when storing your emergency food – this is to make sure that non – food chemicals that are harmful to human health will not transfer. Food grade containers do not contain any chemical that is hazardous to human health. If you are uncertain, find time to reach the manufacture, you can send an email or call them and inquire if it is safe for storing foods.

→ For foods like, pasta, noodles, cereals and other dried foods, you can use different sizes of plastic storage containers. These containers are out of polycarbonate and polyethylene which are especially for dehydrated and dried foods.

→ For storing bulk, dry emergency foods like wheat, rice, beans, oatmeal, flour and sugar, food storage buckets work great.

How to properly seal your plastic food storage container?

Now that you are aware on which and where to keep your emergency food supplies, you now need to learn how to seal your food containers properly. Proper sealing of your food containers will keep it safe from contaminants.

→ Plastic containers or plastic buckets are true oxygen barrier by themselves unlike glass containers or #10 metal cans. The transmission of oxygen through the polyethylene walls of the container is slow but can finally penetrate the containers over time. But there is a common problem with plastic food storage containers, and I bet you've had already experienced this at least maybe once, it is when insect infestation starts due to the prolonged food storage.

✓ There are few remedies for these common issues. You can increase stability and the shelf life of your dry food products, by simple using any of the following items, or both, your food containers before sealing.

✓ You can use an Oxygen absorber packets and or Desiccant Packets. But you need to remember that the oxygen absorbers and desiccant packets are not edible, they are only intended to keep your dry goods dry and to help keep it in a safe condition.

✓ You can use Oxygen barrier bags, may it be plastic or metal. Metalized oxygen barrier bags are best for light and insect control.

✓ Food Grade Diatomaceous Earth (fossil – shell – four), this is entirely organic and edible; it is for preventing organic insect infestation. When you apply this to beans or grains for bulk storage; apply a cup to each 25 pounds of grain to treat it.

Foods to consider during emergencies

Canned Food Items

- Meals: stew, chowder, chili, ravioli, spaghetti, chow mien.
- Fruits: natural juices, not in heavy syrup are advisable.
- Protein: packed in water are advisable.
- Vegetables: beans, peas, corn, carrots, tomatoes (whole, purees and sauce), etc.

Dehydrated items

- Pasta like spaghetti, macaroni and cheese, lasagna.
- Soups and soup mixes.

Staples

- Flour, sugar, cocoa, cornmeal, powdered milk.
- Salt, pepper, seasonings and spices.

- Rice, uncooked cereals.

- Breakfast cereals.

- Vinegar, baking soda.

- Cooking oil.

- Crackers.

- Vitamins.

- Instant beverages like tea, hot chocolate, cider and coffee.

- Condiments.

- Special diet foods for the elderly, infants, diabetics and those with allergies.

- Foods, which are high energy like peanut butter.

- Comfort foods like candies, cookies, hard candies and nuts.

- Simple medical supplies like pain killers, antiseptics, band aids, allergy medicines, Anti-diarrhea medicines, etc.

Chapter 4

How to Can Your Fresh Food and Other Ways of Preserving Your Fresh Food

Ways of Preserving Your Fresh Food

There are several primary techniques on how you can preserve foods inexpensively, by freezing, canning or drying techniques. Modern-day methods of preserving food will help you can and maintain with ease. After understanding the simple and necessary procedures of methods in preserving food, you then need to concentrate on preparing the recipes. By following these suggested ways of preserving your foods, you can surely have money back to your pocket.

Canning

First, we have canning; this is a process in which you are going to apply heat in the food sealed in a jar. In this manner, you are destroying any organism that may cause food spoilage. Usage of proper techniques in canning will stop the spoilage, this happens by just heating the food for a particular period; killing all the unwanted organism. During the process of canning, air is driven out from the jar and a vacuum is formed during the cooling and sealing process.

Canning or preserving food in jars is still one of the easiest ways to preserve small foods such as vegetables and sauces

You might be wondering how to can your food; well, you don't have to search the web anymore because we will teach you simple and easy steps on how to can your foods at home.

→ ***Water-bath canning:*** A technique that is also referred to as *hot water canning,* this method uses a boiling water in a large kettle. Jars that are full are being fully submerged into the water and heated to an internal temperature of 212 ° for a specific duration of time.

Fruit juices, jellies, jams, fruits and other fruit spreads, salsas tomatoes with added acid, sauces, pickles and condiments, this is the ideal method to use.

How to do a water bath canning?

1. Read through recipe and instruction – Prepare the ingredients and equipment. Follow the guideline for the jar size, recipe preparation, and the processing time and of course the preserving method.

2. Quality check – Check jars, lids, and bands to ensure the functionality. Jars with irregular rims, cracks, nicks or even sharp edges may prevent sealing or worst it may lead to jar breakage. The underside lids should not be uneven or have incomplete sealing compound as this may result to unsealed jars. Make sure that the band fits your jar perfectly.

3. Washing – Wash jars, lids and bands in hot soapy water, rinse well. Then dry.

4.   Place the jars in hot water, not in boiling water until it's ready for use. To do it, you need to fill a large saucepan or a stockpot half-way with water. Ensure that the jars are fully submerged, leaving them full of hot water. You may also use dishwashers to wash and heat jars. Keep the jars hot when adding the hot food; this will prevent the jars from breaking. Leave the bands and lids in a room temperature for easy handling.

5.   Prepare tested preserving recipes using fresh produce and other quality ingredients.

6.   Take off the jars from the hot water using a jar lifter; make sure to empty the water inside. The jars should be filled one at a time with the prepared food, and don't forget to leave headspace.

7.   It's advisable to remove the air bubbles. You can use either a bubble remover and a headspace tool or a rubber spatula and slide it between the jar and the food to release the trapped air. Repeat it 2 – 3 times.

8.   Clean the mason jars with a damp cloth to remove any food residue. You can now proceed with applying the bands, and make sure it's tightly sealed.

9.   Put the filled jars in the canner until canner is full. Nest Lower rack with jars into the water; ensure the jars are all covered with water 1 – 2 inches.

10.   Lids are to place in the water bath canners. Then bring the water to a full rolling boil.

11.   Process the jars in the boiling water with the indicated processing time, when the process is complete, you can now turn the cover off and remove the canner lid. Let the jars stand in the canners for around 5 – 6 minutes to get it acclimated to the outside temperature.

12.   Take away the jars from the canner and set it upright on a towel to prevent the jar from breaking that may be caused by the sudden change of the temperature. Leave the jars undisturbed for 24 hours.

13.   Lastly, check the lids for seals. It should not flex up or down when the center is being pressed. Now it's time to remove the bands, and then try lifting off the lids with your fingertips, it has a good seal when the lid cannot be lifted off. However, if the lid does not seal in 24 hours, you can still refrigerate or reprocess the product.

14.   Clean the lids and mason jars.

15.   Label it and make sure to store it in a cold, dark and dry spot for up to a year.

→   ***Pressure canning:*** In this method of canning, you will need a large kettle that produces steam in a locked compartment. The jar filled should be reach temperature of 240° internally under a particular pressure measured by a dial gauge – canner cover. Pressure canning is an ideal method for processing vegetables and low acid foods such as meat, poultry and fish.

How to do the pressure canning

1.   Ready the pressure canner as needed, jars, lids, ring bands, and other helpful accessories.

2.   Washing – Wash jars, lids and bands in hot soapy

water, rinse well. Then dry.

3.   Heat the jar in hot water until it's ready for use. To do it, you need to fill a large saucepan or a stockpot halfway with water. Make sure that the jars are all under water. When placed in water, leaving them full of hot water not boiling water. You may also use dishwashers to wash and boil jars. Keep the jar hot while adding the food, this will prevent the jars from breaking. Leave the bands and lids in a room temperature for easy handling.

4.   Fill the clean hot jars one at a time. You can consider reheating the jars if necessary, simply by immersing the jar in the canning kettle that is full of hot water.

5.   Remember to leave at least an inch headspace, this will allow the expansion of the food. Remove any air pockets by inserting a knife blade along the edge, moving it around the jar.

6.   Take off the air bubbles. You can use either a bubble remover and a headspace tool or a rubber spatula and slide it between the jar and the food to release the trapped air. Repeat it 2 – 3 times.

7.   By using a clean damp cloth, carefully wipe the jar rim. Any food residues in the rim may prevent the sealing process to be successful.

8.   Now it's time to remove lids from the hot water the carefully place it on the jar. Plunge the lids into cold water, if the lids stick together; then dip them again in boiling water. Using your hands, Screw the ring bands as tightly as you comfortably can.

9.   A rack should be in the canner and filled half full with hot water. Make sure the jar is full of with hot not boiling water.

10.   Place jars on a rack so the steam can flow around while processing jars of food.

11.   Securely fasten the canner lids.

12.   Heat it to the highest setting until the steam flows from the vent port or petcock.

13.   Maintain the setting in high heat, exhaust steam for about 10 minutes more or a little less and close the petcock. It will pressurize for the next 3 to 5 minutes.

14.   Start timing the process and watch out until the dial gauge shows that it has reached recommended pressure.

15.   The weighted gauges should rock about 2 to three times per minute. For presto canners, they should rock slowly during the entire process.

16.   You can now turn the heat off once finished. Remove the canner from heat to let the canner depressurize.

17.   Never force- cool canners. Force - cooling will just result to food spoilage or loss of liquid from the jars.

18.   Once the canner depressurized, open the petcock. And then wait for about 2 minutes, unfasten the lid and carefully remove it. Imperative to keep the lid away from your face, so it won't burn.

19.   Take off the jars from the canner and set it upright on a towel to prevent the jar from breaking that may be caused by the sudden change of the temperature. Leave the jars undisturbed for 24 hours.

20.   Lastly, check the lids for seals. It should not flex up or down when the center is being pressed. Now it's time to remove the bands, and then try lifting off the lids with your fingertips, it has a good seal when the lid cannot be lifted off. However, if the lid does not seal in 24 hours, you can still refrigerate or reprocess the product.

21.   Label it and make sure to store it in a cold, dark, and dry area for up to a year.

Drying

The oldest method in preserving foods is the drying process, in which food are exposed to a high temperature. It is the temperature that is high enough to remove the moisture from the food, but will not cook it. Good air circulation is a big help in drying the food evenly. Most dried items include fish, nuts and meat.

How to dry foods at home

→ **Sun Drying;** it is safe to dry food under the sun, aside from being safe, sun drying is a very economical way of preserving food especially fruits. However, Meats and vegetables cannot be dried outdoors since they have low acid content and low sugar. Unlike fruits, fruits have high acid content and high sugar, which makes sun drying easy and safe. Vegetables and meats are best dried indoors with the use of a dehydrator or controlled oven since humidity and temperature are essential during food preservation.

Fish being dried in the sun in Madagascar

You should have a constant breeze and of course a warm temperature in order to dry foods in the sun. 85° F is the minimum temperature which is necessary for the sun drying process but, of course, higher temperature is obviously better. The high temperature will extract the moisture from the food while the breeze will help to dispel it into the surrounding air. Humidity of 60° is ideal, however high humidity level in the South make sun drying difficult; to have a successful sun drying process a low level of humidity is important.

Sun drying is slow, and time-consuming because the weather is uncontrollable or unpredictable which is the dying agent.

1. Prepare the equipment needed in the sun drying process. You'll need a rack or screen that will be a place on a particular surface or an aluminum sheet. This arrangement will ensure an adequate airflow around the food. Placing the racks or screens on top of concrete sur-

faces or aluminum sheets will help in increasing the temperature that will make the process a bit faster.

2.   Make sure to use food-grade quality materials for the racks or screens, Screens made of Teflon – coated fiberglass, stainless steel or plastic are the ideals for sun drying. Avoid screens made of copper, hardware cloth or aluminum which is galvanized metal coated with zinc or cadmium which is hazardous to human health.

3.   Protect the drying fruits from insects and birds, you can use some covering to protect your food that is on the process of sun drying. You can just use another screen, or you can use a clean cheese cloth to cover the fruits.

4.   Leave the fruit under the sun, and gather once they are entirely dried up. This process may take a while.

→   ***Drying Food Indoors;*** with the help of modern gadgets, Indoor food drying was made easier, Gadgets such as conventional ovens, counter top conventional ovens and dehydrators. You can dry herbs and other foods with the use of a microwave oven because the air flow there isn't adequate.

Food Dehydrators – This is usually a small electrical appliance used in drying foods indoor. Dehydrators have an electric element that produces heat, and a fan that helps out with the air circulation. A lot of dehydrators; designed for  drying foods at 140°F, which makes them efficient and quick.

You can buy a food dehydrator from department stores, natural food stores, catalogues and some of the garden supplies stores. The price ranges from $50 up to $350 depending on the features.

Chapter 5

Strategies to Help You Properly Manage Your Food and Water In The Event Of an Emergency

How to Manage Your Food Supply Effectively?

It is important to know managing your food and water supply during emergencies to effectively utilize its use. There might be a need to survive on your own after an emergency. It means having your water, food and other kinds of supplies in sufficient amount that should last for a minimum of 72 hours. After any disaster, relief workers and local officials will be on the scene, but you can't be sure that they'll reach you first. You could get help in few hours or maybe it may take days.

Essential services such as gas, electricity, sewage treatment, water and telephone connection may be down for days or maybe longer. Your survival kit should have items that will help you during these outages. Every 6-12 months food and water should be rotated and use by dates should be followed to make sure that food and water is safe to drink. Store canned goods in a cool, dry place, about 40-60 F to prevent it from spoiling. Keep a food protected from insects and rodents by storing in air tight containers. Do not eat canned goods that have become swollen, dented, or corroded. In the case of a power outage, eat foods in the refrigerator first, then from the freezer, and then from storage. In a well-insulated freezer, foods can be in good condition up to two days if there are ice crystals in the center of the food. Food can remain in good condition up to 4 hours if the fridge is unopened.

Consume only what you need. You have to remember that relief goods might be a delay for a while, so might as well utilize your supplies effectively.

Right knowledge on how to manage your food during an emergency is the key to survival. Here are some more tips that will surely help you in managing your supply during disasters.

→   Allow each individual to drink according to their needs. – The water that our body need depends on our age, physical condition, the time of the year, and of course physical activities.

→   Make sure you turn off your house's main water valves – This is to avoid the water from contamination.

→   You must be knowledgeable in determining if the water is safe or not.

→   You should be flexible in cooking foods with the available implements.   Can goods can be eaten right after opening, but you can still heat it by just removing the label, disinfecting and washing the can with diluted solution of a part bleach to 10 pans of water. Remember to open the can first before heating.

→   Look for alternative places where you can keep your perishable goods to lengthen their life if there is a power outage; perhaps, you can bury foods under the ground and the snow.

Avoid using powdered formulas with treated water, it is safer to use pre-prepared canned baby formulas, when feeding your baby.

Chapter 6

How to Effectively Scavenge and Restock Your Supplies

Finding Water Sources

Alternative sources of clean and potable water found inside and outside your house, never drink water that has a strange odor or unusual color, or if you think that the water has contaminants. Don't risk your health. The following are possible water sources in case of emergency in which you ran out of water to drink:

Inside the Home

- Melted Ice cubes, but make sure that it's from clean water.
- Water from your house's water heater tank
- Water from your house's toilet tank, nut from the bowl. Make sure the water is exceptionally clear and not treated with any chemical.
- The juice took from the canned fruit or vegetables.

Outside the Home

- Water from Rainwater
- Water from Streams, rivers, and other bodies of water
- Water from Ponds and lakes
- Water from Natural springs

Water from sources outside the home should be treated .as described in Chapter 2.

Food Sources

The best way to find food sources is to store food. You never know until when an emergency could last. Dried foods will last longer than moist foods. Utilize your food sources well, so you don't have to scavenge food sources that much. Before a disaster strikes, go to places where people don't, usually, go for their primary source of water and food supplies after the warning and up until close to the time of calamity occurrence. As the panic level increase and more people run to the main source of food and shopping centers, supplies by then become less and less available. Never risk going outside during disaster. After a disaster and when your food reserves are low, go to places less frequented for food. As surviving is, the goal and calories are the keys.

.

Conclusion

Preparedness is still the best resort during emergencies. Many of us does not seem to observe preparedness during disasters, but being able to put things in order before any disaster could put us way too far than those who do not prepare. It gives us an edge to keep track of things and make us ready to face such emergencies. Should there be any calamity befall you and your family, it may change your current situation into one of survival. You do know what to do, where to go, how to get off there, how to provide food and water for yourself and loved ones. You'll know what will you need and how much. Preparation will indeed potentially help you one day.

Most of us don't stress the importance on making preparations during emergencies. We have been victims to various disasters, and it seems like we do not learn at all. This book explores strategies and skills in preparing for emergencies like natural disasters and power shortages. It provides information on possible things you can do to store food and water during emergencies. It includes ideas on food preservation, proper water storage and other emergency-related tips. Food preservation like canning and drying were also discussed to help further the reader with ideas on other ways to avoid food spoilage during emergencies. In the current world technology, we seem to be so relaxed that we do not put much care on emergency-related preparations, but like what the saying sometimes go, "Prevention is always better than cure." Preparation is indeed the best way to lessen the effect of disasters in our lives and might save us from further damages or tragedies.

From The Author

Thank you for taking the time to read this book. As an author, I understand the importance of creating books which my readers will find both enjoyable and informative. If you have the time and feel generous, please don't hesitate to leave an honest review of this book..........*Ron Johnson*

No...I insist...Thank You!

Other Books By Ron Johnson

RV Living For Beginners

Are You Fed Up Of Working The 9-5 To Pay The Mortgage Or Rent Plus The Bills And Considering Leaving It All Behind And Hitting The Road?

When you want to change your lifestyle entirely, you need to have enough motivation but you also need to have knowledge about the lifestyle that you are adopting. Many people who want to live in an RV full-time fail to find a balance in their lives which make that living pleasurable, while others can live the dream and learn to compromise on comforts for the sake of freedom. They wake up in the mornings to feel that they have breathed fresh air. They see different scenery every morning if they so wish. What you need to know before joining them is whether you're cut out for the lifestyle and what differences there are between living in a conventional home and living in an RV. This book bridges that gap in your knowledge, and although you may choose to save a fortune by staying at home, you may also choose the lesser travelled road and discover the benefits of living in an RV.

Both lifestyles, either in an RV or a home, have their pros and cons. Many who choose the RV lifestyle find that adapting their lives comes naturally. It takes a unique and free spirited person to compromise on the luxuries of home living in favor of the adventurous lifestyle offered by RV living, though many do. Once you weigh the pros and cons, you can make the choice wisely, and that's what this book is all about. The book will appeal to the free spirited who seek something more than merely surviving month to month oppressed by bills, mortgage payments and housing taxes.

Both have benefits, though those who live the life they choose, rather than the life chosen for them by responsibility, find that RV life tests their personal boundaries and skills freeing up their lives to live beyond the grid. Journey with us and learn if living in an RV will suit you, and be prepared for the journey of your life.

The Prepper's Guide To Grid Down Survival

Are you ready to live through a long term downed power grid situation?

Many people don't stop to think how they will eat, get clean drinking water or stay warm when the power goes out. This book covers some of the most plausible scenarios as well as how you will manage during the grid failure.

You need to think about how you will maintain personal hygiene, take care of toilet issues and feed your family as well as how you will keep them safe and warm. You don't know how much you rely on electricity until it is ripped away from you. It can leave your entire world turned upside down if you are not ready. It is hard to imagine and prepare for every little thing without doing some research first. This book will hold your hand and help you come up with a plan that will get you through a long lasting grid failure. Planning and preparing can help remove the fear that is associated with the unknown. Get your family involved and start your preparations with the help of the information in this book.

The Death Of Money

"It is well enough that people of the nation do not understand our banking and monetary system, for if they did, I believe there would be a revolution before tomorrow morning"..................Henry Ford, 1922

It isn't hard to see that the economies in almost every country are in bad shape. There are constantly reports of this big bank falling or that big business going bankrupt. In fact, in the United States, entire cities are either in bankruptcy or on the verge. What happens when a city goes bankrupt? Millions of dollars that are owed to various creditors would never be paid back. Those creditors would take a major hit and could be forced to go under as well. The chain reaction would be devastating and could ultimately result in the complete devastation of fiat paper currency.

Are you prepared to live in a world where fiat paper money holds no value? You wouldn't have a job and if you did, you would be paid with credits or with gold or silver pieces. It is unfathomable to think of a world where we can't run to the store and use our debit cards to buy groceries or pay cash for medical services. If and when paper money becomes worthless, citizens all around the world are going to have to adopt a new way of living.

In order to survive an economic collapse, people are going to have to rely on themselves. There will be no government bailouts. There will be no government aid. You will have to learn how to hunt, grow a garden and raise livestock in order to feed your family. You can help offset the upheaval by stocking up on some things today that will make that bleak tomorrow look a little better. This book will explain what you need to start buying today as well as teach you the new form of tender—bartering. You will also learn about the history of paper money and how history tells us it always fails at some point. Will you be ready?

www.ingramcontent.com/pod-product-compliance
Lightning Source LLC
Chambersburg PA
CBHW070513290526
45790CB00003B/1214